First drafts don't have to be perfect – just finished!

No part of this book may be reproduced or transmitted in any form or by any means, graphic, electronic, or mechanical, including photocopying, recording, taping, or by any informational storage retrieval system without advanced prior permission in writing from the publisher

Copyright February 2020 © Emilia Edwards

Grateful thanks to Shutterstock and Anna Poguliaeva for the lovely cover image.

About this book

I've presented 41 different prompts here to encourage you to focus on different aspects of writing, whether it be tense, point of view (POV), or using your senses to describe a scene, or to spot and begin developing plot ideas.

You will see each new prompt at the top of the page, and there will be three pages for you to write the piece for that prompt. If you need more room, by all means, write on separate pages and attach them to this book, or write all the prompts in a separate book.

You might find that once you've done a few of these, and got into the habit of writing, that you'd like to go back and have another go at some of the early ones. Do that. It will be helpful for you to revisit already completed pieces and see what you might do differently, or just try to tackle it from a different standpoint.

As much as possible write the whole piece for each prompt in one continuous session. Allow about twenty to thirty minutes for each. Read the prompt, then think for a minute or two before you begin writing. If you really get inspired and need to keep writing after twenty or thirty minutes, for goodness' sake, don't stop!

When writing, don't stop to edit your spelling or alter wording. Just keep writing until you've finished. Wait until a piece is finished before editing it, if you want to do that. You may even find it helpful to leave a piece for a few weeks before rereading it. It will seem fresh and you will be able to view it more objectively after a break.

Happy writing!

1. Look at yourself in a mirror. Describe what you see as if talking about a stranger.

2. What was the first thing you ate and drank this morning? What was it, how did you get it, how did it look, smell, taste and feel?

3. What does this picture say to you?
Write about it.

4. Tell someone from another planet how to do the dishes. And why!

5. Write about a teacher from school you really disliked.

6. Describe your perfect romantic first date

7. Describe your dinner as if you were a fancy food critic.

8. Write your earliest memory, but as if it happened to someone else, ie in the third person not first person.

9. Imagine you painted the Mona Lisa. Why did you choose that particular person to paint?

10. Describe a cricket or baseball match without using the words hit, bat or plate/wicket.

11. Write a piece that includes at least four of these objects: a rainbow; a baby's dummy/pacifier; a broken umbrella; an empty can; a broken fingernail; a paper tissue.

12. Write about a day in the life of a prehistoric man.

13. Describe taking a bath or shower, but you can only use the senses of smell and hearing. No touch, taste or sight.

14. What does this picture say to you?
Write about it.

15. Write a short piece beginning with the phrase, 'It was half past seven on a Wednesday morning, and the bus was already crowded...'

16. Imagine you are the only journalist to interview the first man to walk on the moon. What are you going to ask him?

17. The last geese fly overhead, migrating for the winter. How do you feel?

18. Write about a spider spinning a web, without using the word gossamer, or the word silk.

19. What does this picture say to you?
Write about it.

20. Describe kissing someone you love.

21. You have to climb a ladder, but you're terrified of heights. What happens? How do you feel?

22. What's worse, a doctor's appointment or a dentist's? Why?

23. Which five books would you save first from your home if it caught fire? (Your family and pets are safe!) Why those five books?

24. What does this picture say to you? Write about it.

25. Someone you hated dies, and you go to the funeral. What happens? How do you feel?

26. Picture yourself walking round your old school at night. What happens? How do you feel?

27. Imagine you are the first man to walk on the moon. You are being interviewed. What will you say? (Should be an easy one after exercise 16!)

28. A good friend has disappeared, no one has seen or heard from them for four days, but their family don't seem bothered. What do you do?

29. Write a conversation between two guys having a drink. Don't use the words 'he said' or 'he replied'.

30. What does this picture say to you? Write about it.

31. You meet your Ex and they are with a new partner and seem very happy. What happens? How do you feel?

32. Describe a cup of coffee (or your beverage of choice). Engage all your senses here.

33. Describe either a hot sunny day for a funeral, or a cold wet day for a wedding.

34. Close your eyes and imagine moving around your house. Pretend you are telling someone else how to find their way around your house, from the kitchen to the bedroom, to the living room and then the bathroom. Remember any bends, corners and other obstacles.

35. Your friend turns up at your house sober and neatly dressed. They tell you they are God. How does this conversation go?

36. You wake suddenly in the middle of the night. Something or someone is in your house. The power is off. What do you do?

37. What does this picture say to you? Write about it.

38. Write a short piece about Summer using only words of four and five letters.

39. Describe snow to someone who has never seen it.

40. What does this picture say to you? Write about it.

41. Using **at least** four of these write a short piece about a school reunion: bully; truant; dance; History paper; a broken heel; a chameleon.

Hey!

You made it!

I hope you got something out of this, and that using these exercises has given you more confidence to work on your own writing projects, or maybe helped you to develop a routine for writing.

You can create your own prompts by looking at a variety of sources, such as pins on Pinterest, images on stock image sites such as Pixabay, 'people-watching': observing people or listening to conversations when you're out and about (just don't be too obvious – you don't want to get a punch on the nose!), or by looking up quotes or just turning to a random page in any book and using a one-line snippet to start you off.

The main thing is, to keep writing, as that is the only way anyone can really learn how to write.

Happy writing and thank you!

Printed in Great Britain
by Amazon